## ·HIDDEN WORLDS·
### HEATHER AMERY·JANE SONGI

# IN THE
# HOME

# ·HIDDEN WORLDS·
## HEATHER AMERY·JANE SONGI

# IN THE
# HOME

## MARVELS THROUGH THE MICROSCOPE

HAMLYN

**Editor:** Julia Gorton
**Designer:** Hugh Schermuly
**Picture Researcher:** Emily Hedges
**Production Controller:** Ruth Charlton

First published in 1993 by Hamlyn Children's Books,
an imprint of Reed International Books Limited,
Michelin House, 81 Fulham Road, London SW3 6RB,
and Auckland, Melbourne, Singapore and Toronto.

This paperback edition published in 1994.

**ISBN 0 600 58432 1**

Cataloguing-in-Publication Data.
A catalogue record for this book is available from the British Library.

Printed in Italy

# CONTENTS

# INTRODUCTION

When you look closely, you can see all sorts of small things - a grain of sugar, a tiny insect or a speck of dust. With a magnifying glass, which is a glass lens, you can see much more detail.

Microscopes, which have several glass lenses, were invented nearly 400 years ago. For the first time, scientists could see the germs which cause disease, the countless cells in our blood, and millions of other things that no-one knew existed. Microscopes today can magnify an object up to 2,000 times its normal size.

We can now look even closer with electron microscopes, which were invented about 60 years ago. Instead of light, these microscopes use a beam of electrons to "look" at tiny things, and can magnify up to 250,000 times.

This researcher is using a scanning electron microscope to examine a tiny object. The pictures show up on a television screen.

This technician is using a light microscope to study samples of bacteria.

Look closely at a spoonful of sugar and you can see that each grain is a roughly-shaped crystal.

Sugar as we usually see it.

Magnified 2.5 times, a collection of glass-like crystals.

At 50 times their normal size, are these crystals or boulders?

This is how the corner of one crystal looks when it is magnified 500 times.

# IN THE
# HOME

# Fleece and Fibre

**T**ake a close look at a thick woollen jumper and you will see that each of the wool threads bristles with many tiny fibres. The same is true of other threads made from natural fibres, such as cotton, although they are not as easy to see without a microscope. Fibres which come from plants and animals are short and very thin. Before they can be used, they have to be twisted together, or spun, to make long lengths of strong thread for knitting or weaving.

*Close-up on cotton* (left). When someone wears a cotton shirt for just one day, the collar gets dirty, even if that person does wash his or her neck properly. By the end of the day, the woven threads are matted with grease, sweat, dust and tiny pieces of rubbed-off skin.

After a good hot wash in a washing machine, with lots of detergent, the threads of the collar are clean and separate.

**Single thread, many fibres** (right). This is a close view of a thread of cotton going through the eye of a needle. It shows the many thin fibres which make up a single thread of sewing cotton.

**Dirty collar**
(x 25)

**Clean collar**
(x 25)

**Needle and thread**
(x 25)

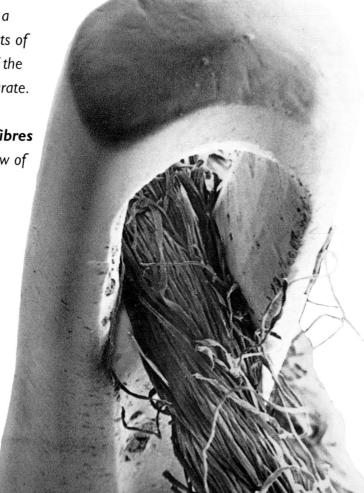

**Wool for warmth.** Sheep's wool is full of natural oil, dirt, specks of earth and bits of grass and seeds. When the fleece is cut off, it is very greasy and lumpy. Different parts of the fleece have a different feel - in some places, the wool is long and rough while in others it is short and fine. Each type of wool is cut off and sorted into the different kinds. It is then washed thoroughly and dried.

The clean wool is pulled apart to get rid of the lumps and then combed to make all the fibres lie one way. Next it is spun, or twisted, into a long, thin rope. Wool is very strong and can be bent backwards and forwards many times without breaking.

**Sheep**

**Unwashed wool**
*(x 570)*

**Sheep's wool is washed several times to get rid of the dirt and grease before it is ready for spinning.**

**Washed wool**
*(x 560)*

**Knitted sweater**

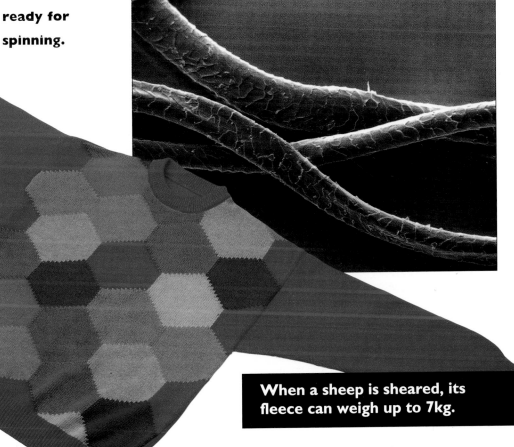

## DID YOU KNOW?

Most wool comes from sheep but the very best and most expensive wool comes from goats. Cashmere is made from the fleece of Kashmir goats which live in northern India and Tibet. Mohair is made from the wool of Angora goats. Camel hair is also made into a soft, warm cloth.

**When a sheep is sheared, its fleece can weigh up to 7kg.**

# Chemical Cloth

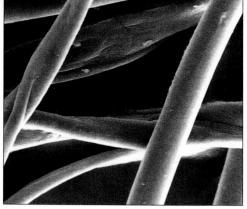

**Cotton and polyester**
(x 1,130)

If you look at the labels in the clothes you are wearing, you may find that they are made of things like nylon, polyester, acrylic and viscose. All of these fibres are made in factories. They are often used to make carpets, curtains, sheets and blankets, as well as clothing. Man-made fibres do not rot or get eaten by moths, like natural fibres, and they are often stronger.

*Mix and match* (above). *Natural and man-made fibres are often mixed together to weave many different kinds of cloth. Polyester on its own is very slippery and cotton creases easily. A mixture of the two gets over both problems.*

*This is a mixture of cotton and polyester. The round fibres are polyester and the flat, twisted ones are cotton. The sheets on your bed may be made of this fabric. It is strong, easy to wash and dry and doesn't need ironing.*

Nylon tights are knitted by machines. The machines loop the very long, thin nylon threads together to make a kind of mesh.

(x 55)

(x 160)

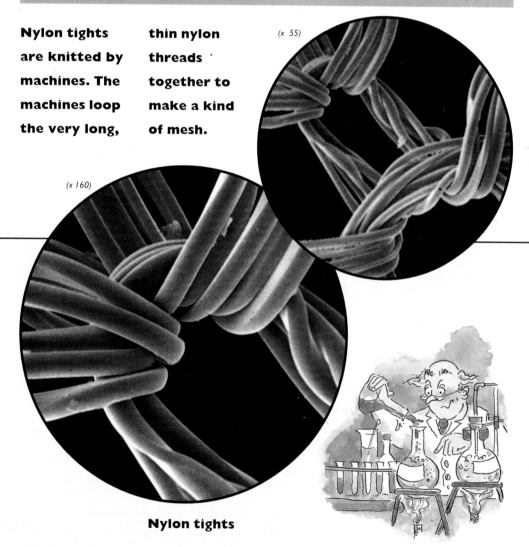

**Nylon tights**

## Man-made mesh

Nylon is made by mixing two complicated chemicals together. The nylon is then a liquid. It is forced through tiny holes in a machine and comes out as dry, very thin, long strands. The strands are twisted together into threads, stretched and wound on to bobbins. They are then ready to be woven or knitted into clothes, tights and other things.

**Stretching out** *(below). Lycra is the trade name for a shiny manufactured fibre. It is made from oil and lots of chemicals. When it is woven into fabric, it is very stretchy and hard-wearing. It also washes well and dries quickly. It is especially good for making tight-fitting sports clothes, such as swimming costumes, cycling shorts and leotards.*

*This is a close-up of a pair of cycling shorts. They are made of lycra sandwiched between two layers of nylon. The lycra is the yellowy orange threads and the nylon is the red and green ones.*

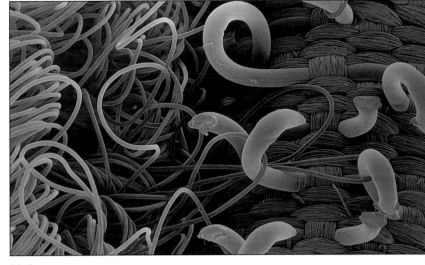

**Velcro**
*(x 11)*

**Lycra**
*(x 30)*

**Velcro is made of nylon. One side is covered with tiny hooks. The other has lots of loops. When the two sides meet, the hooks catch in the loops and hold them together.**

**Wood, oil and even milk can be used to make man-made fibres.**

## Fighting fat

People who like very sweet tea may put on weight. Instead of sugar, they use artificial sweetening tablets. These are made of chemicals. They taste very sweet but are not fattening. One sweetener, called saccharine, is made from coal.

Chemical sweeteners are put into diet fizzy drinks as well as lots of prepared foods.

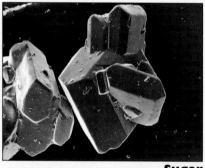

**Sugar**
(x 50)

**Saccharine**
(x 45)

# One Spoon or Two?

Tea with salt and rancid yak's butter? Or perhaps with spearmint leaves stirred in? A refreshing cup of tea is enjoyed by many people all over the world, but not always with milk and sugar.

Tea has been grown in China and Japan for thousands of years. It was first brought to Europe about 300 years ago and was very expensive. Later it was grown in India and is now produced in about 30 countries in Asia and Africa.

*Natural sweetness.* Sugar comes from the sap of sugar cane or from sugar beet. Sugar cane grows in hot countries which have plenty of rain. The cane looks like bamboo and grows up to 3m high. After the cane is cut, the sap is collected and dried to make the sugar crystals.

Sugar beet is a root which is grown in cooler countries. The beets are crushed to extract the sweet juice. It is then processed and dried into crystals.

***Dried-leaf drink*** *(below). Tea leaves come from small trees or bushes that grow best on hot, sunny hillsides where there is plenty of rain. When the leaves are picked, they are a dark, shiny green. They are then dried in factories or in the sun and go black or brown. They are crushed to break up the dried leaves, fermented and dried again.*

*Tea made with Chinese leaves is usually weak and pale. Tea from India and Africa is often stronger and darker. Different leaves are mixed together to make teas which have special tastes and colours. There are over 1,500 different blends of tea.*

**Milk powder is made by drying milk to get rid of the water. It does not taste like fresh milk but it keeps for months and is very light to carry about.**

**Dried milk powder**
*(x 300)*

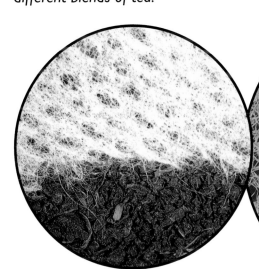

**Teabag perforations**
*(x 7)*

**Tea leaves, pressed into blocks, were once used as money in China.**

**Tea and teabag**
*(x 3)*

**Tea bags are made of man-made fibres. Each bag has up to 2,000 tiny holes to let out the colour and taste of the tea leaves.**

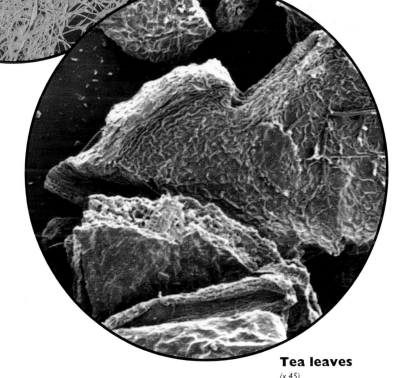

**Tea leaves**
*(x 45)*

# Snack Time

**M**any of the things we like to eat are not quite as simple as they look. The sweet juicy parts of a fruit are often just covers for the seeds or stone inside it. When birds or animals eat the fruit, they may carry the seeds or stones away from the plant or tree. Then the seeds or stones grow into new plants or trees and produce more fruit. We often eat raw fruit but many foods have to be cooked or processed before they are good to eat.

## DID YOU KNOW?

Nuts are fruits. The biggest is the coconut. When a nut drops from a palm tree into the sea, its thick shell keeps it afloat. It may be blown by the wind for hundreds of kilometres before being washed up on a beach. There it may grow into a new coconut palm.

*Protective peel. Many fruits have a tough skin or peel which are not good to eat. The skin protects them from moulds and fungus which feed on the fruit and make it go bad or rotten.*

*Waxy and furry skins make the fruit waterproof. This stops insects from landing on the fruit when it is wet and from burrowing into it. When the skin is broken or split, perhaps by a bird pecking it or when it is too ripe, then insects, mould and fungus can get in. The waxy skins on apples help them to stay in good condition for weeks and even months after they have been picked from the trees and stored.*

Peaches have furry skins. This close-up of a peach shows the hairs growing on the skin. The small bumps are young hairs.

**The longest peel, cut from one apple, was longer than two tennis courts.**

Peaches and strawberries

*A **sprinkling of crystals**. Salt is a chemical which is made up of tiny crystals. It comes from sea water or is dug out from underground mines. In some hot countries, huge flat pans are filled with sea water and left to dry in the sun. When the water has evaporated, pure salt is left behind.*

*The salt you put on your food is pure salt with a chemical added to it. This keeps it dry so that it pours easily. Without the chemical, the salt takes in moisture from the air and becomes damp, sticky lumps.*

**Salt crystals**
*(x 22)*

**Peach skin**
*(x 650)*

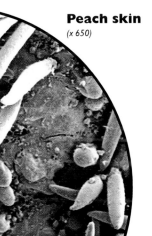

Most fruits have their stones or pips on the inside.

But a straw-berry's tiny brown seeds are found on its surface.

**Table salt**
*(x 32)*

Potato crisps are very thin slices of potato which are salted and baked with fat in an oven.

The holes you can see in this crisp are little pockets of air.

**Strawberry skin**
*(x 17)*

**Potato crisp**
*(x 50)*

**When you bite a crisp, the air pockets explode and help to make the crunch.**

13

# Friends and Fiends

Mouldy bread

Stilton cheese

Rotting apple

Your food is eaten not just by you, but also by creatures so small that you need a microscope to see them. Sometimes these creatures make the food taste or look nasty. For example, some bacteria make milk taste sour and some fungi grow into patches of mould on bread.

There are times, however, when microscopic creatures are added to foods to produce a particular look, taste or smell. Cheeses get their different tastes from the special bacteria and fungi used to make them. Also bread will not rise unless the tiny yeast organism is added to the dough.

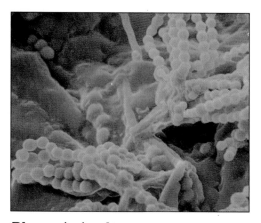

Blue vein in cheese
(x 865)

The blue veins in Stilton and other "blue" cheeses are made by a mould. The mould is put into the cheese to give it a special taste.

**Yeast cells are so small you could lie 800 in a line on one fingernail.**

## A little wine?

Yeast is a type of fungus. When it grows, the tiny cells produce new ones which split off and grow their own new cells.

The white powder on grape skins, called bloom, contains yeast cells. When the grapes are pressed, the yeast goes into the juice. It uses sugar in the juice to make alcohol and turn the juice into wine.

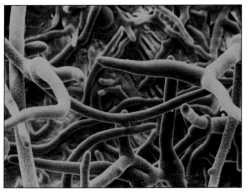

**Bread mould**
*(x 210)*

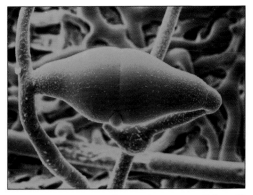

**Growing mould cell**
*(x 275)*

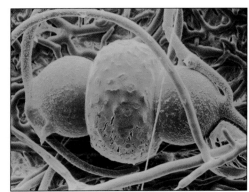

**New mould cell**
*(x 175)*

*Multiplying mould* (above). Mould grows on old bread when it is warm and damp. The mould is a mass of tiny branched tubes. They feed on the bread, spreading across it and burrowing inside.

Sometimes two tubes meet and grow together (above middle). The area where the tubes meet gets larger and then a tyre-shaped swelling forms (above right) containing a new fungus "seed". The seed will produce a new branched tube when it lands on something it can feed on.

**Grapes with bloom**

**Apple mould**
*(x 770)*

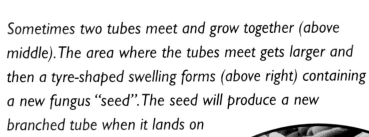

**Yeast cells**
*(x 1,700)*

*Bad apple* (right). An apple goes rotten when a fungus gets through the skin into the fruit. The fungus spreads by growing tubes. Here are many tubes packed closely together. Young yellow fungus is growing out of older green fungus.

15

# Metal Medley

**N**eedles and pins, pots and pans, coins and jewellery, the cars we travel around in - all of these are made from different metals. Metals are mined out of the ground, and are usually mixed in with huge amounts of rock. Once they have been separated out, the metals have to go through several further processes before they can be shaped or moulded.

Most metals rust or tarnish in the damp air. They have to be coated with paint or varnish to stop them rusting, or polished regularly to keep them shiny.

**In the past, valuable coins were made of gold or silver. Now the gold or silver would be worth much more than the coin, so coins today are made of mixtures of cheap metals. Some have ridges round the edges, called milling. You can feel it with your fingers.**

*Stamp of quality* (right). Things made of gold and silver are stamped with special marks, called hallmarks. The hallmarks show that the ring, necklace, spoon or whatever has been tested and contains a certain amount of pure gold or silver. The test is called assaying. A tiny amount of metal is scraped or cut off and tested with special chemicals.

*If you look inside a gold ring, you will usually see a row of four marks. They show the maker's name, the date the ring was made, the quality of the metal and where the ring was tested. The head of a leopard means that the ring was tested for purity in London.*

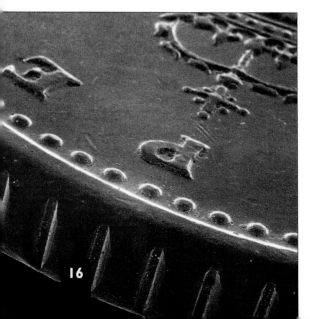

**Coin**
(x 30)

**Hallmark**
(x 40)

***A little rusty*** (below). *The outsides of most cars are made of thin sheets of steel. They are pressed into shape by huge machines in a factory. When a car is finished, it is sprayed with a special hard paint, called cellulose.*

*If water and air get under the cellulose, the steel starts to rust. Small rough brown spots appear on the old car when the rust breaks through the cellulose. Here are layers of blue and green cellulose with the rust underneath.*

  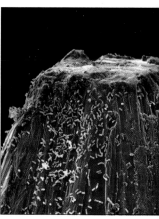

**Needle point**
(x 7)

(x 35)

(x 180)

**A sewing needle is made of steel. The point looks** **very smooth and sharp. With a microscope,** **you can see it is really quite blunt and rough.**

**Rust on car**
(x 45)

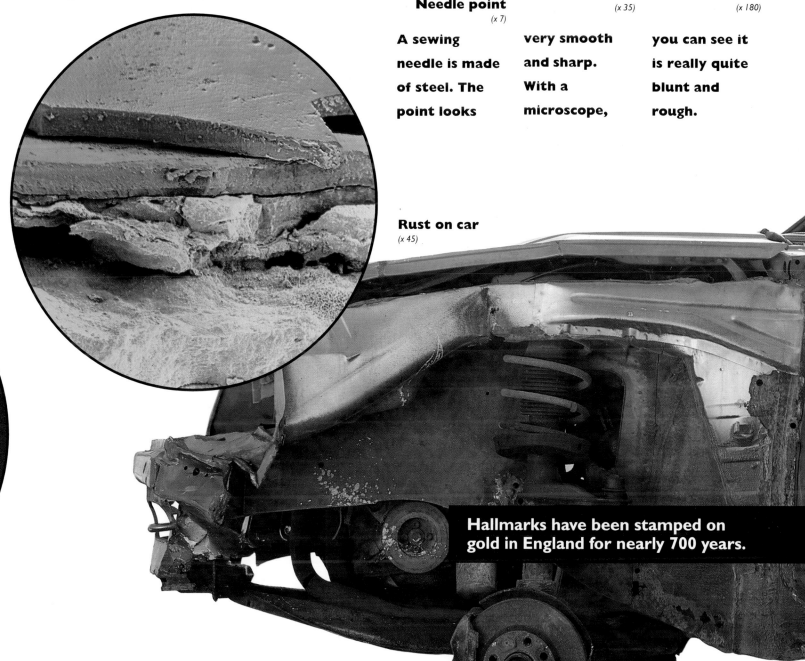

**Hallmarks have been stamped on gold in England for nearly 700 years.**

**Record**

# Sound Secrets

Every noise, from the squeak of a mouse or the voice of a pop singer, to the roar of a jet engine, makes waves which travel through the air. The waves are called vibrations. When the vibrations reach your ears, you hear the mouse, the pop singer or the jet. If the sounds are recorded and played back, you hear them again. A very close look at a record or a compact disc shows how the recording makes the vibrations.

*(x 20)*

*(x 50)*

***In the groove.*** *When a pop star sings into a microphone, the vibrations are changed into electrical signals. These signals control a tiny chisel. It moves slowly around a metal disc, cutting a wavy groove in it. This is called the master disc. The record you buy is a plastic copy of the master disc.*

*When you play the record, a special needle, called a stylus, runs along the wavy groove, which makes it vibrate. The vibrations are turned back into electrical signals. They go to the speakers and come out as a pop song.*

**Stylus in groove**
*(x 525)*

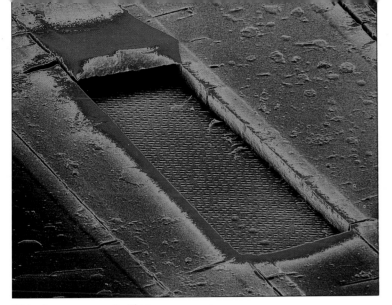

**Pits in compact disc**
(x 275)

**Words and pictures.** *Compact discs can now be used to record pictures as well as sounds. These are played back on a special piece of equipment linked up to an ordinary television set or computer screen.*

**Compact discs have a plastic coating to protect them. A piece of the coating has been taken off this CD to show the tiny pits on the playing surface.**

**Light to sound show.** *Compact discs sold in the shops are copies of the master disc. But instead of a groove, like a record, CDs have a line of billions of tiny pits. These are made on the disc with pulses of brilliant light from a laser.*

*When you play a CD, a much weaker laser beam shines on the tiny pits. As the disc spins round, the pits break up the beam into pulses. These are turned into electrical signals, amplified and fed to the speakers.*

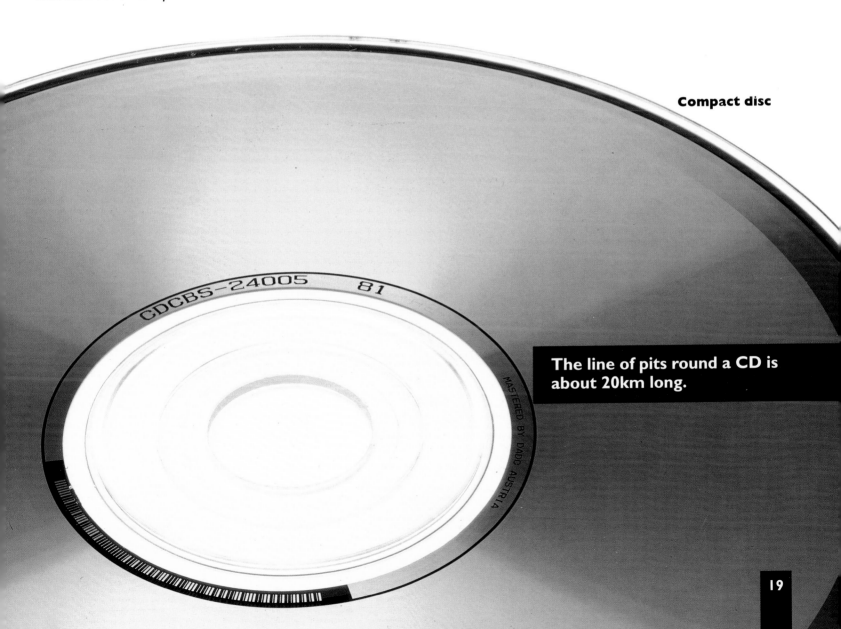

**Compact disc**

CDCBS-24005 81

MASTERED BY DADO AUSTRIA

**The line of pits round a CD is about 20km long.**

# Chips with Everything

All sorts of machines we use every day, from pocket calculators and television sets to microwave ovens and computers use electricity to make them work. Inside them, the electricity goes along special paths, called circuits. Because the circuits are so small, the machines can also be very small.

## DID YOU KNOW?

Microchips are made from very thin slices of silicon. These are printed with circuits, heated and treated with chemicals, then cut up into 6mm squares.

**Printed circuit board**
(x 0.7)

*Colour-coded.* In all sorts of machines, the electricity goes along very complicated circuits to the microchips and other parts, and to the dials and the control knobs. To make very small circuits on special boards, the paths for the electricity are printed on them by using photographs. The unwanted parts are then removed with chemicals, leaving the circuits.

On this board, the pale green and brown lines are paths for the electricity. Other parts, such as wires to microchips, switches and dials will be welded on to the blue dots.

**Ant with microchip**

**One microchip can store all the words of a full-sized book.**

**Wires on a microchip**
*(x 50)*

**Wire welded to microchip**
*(x 400)*

**This microchip has all the wires in place, linking it up to the circuit board.**

**Each wire has a pad, welded to the chip.**

**This ant has been photographed holding a micro-chip. The chip and the ant are about 30 times their real size.**

*Electric pictures.* The pictures you see on a television screen are made up of three colours, red, blue and green. The television camera picks up light from the things it is filming. It divides up the light into the three colours and changes it into electrical signals. The transmitter sends out the signals as radio waves.

When you switch on the television, it picks up the radio waves, and turns them into electrical signals. The pictures that you watch are built up by three coloured electron beams. They scan across the screen, line by line, so quickly that you do not notice them - all you see are the pictures.

**Television screen**

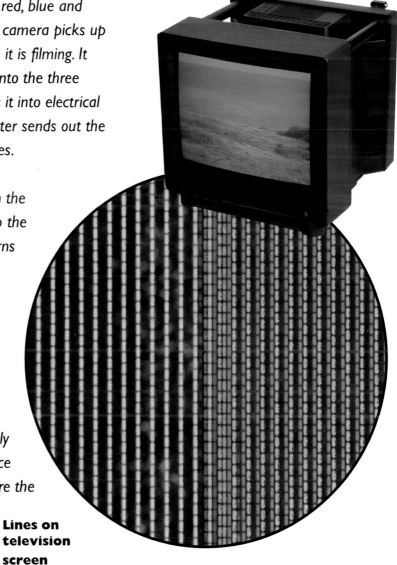

**Lines on television screen**

# Dining on Dirt

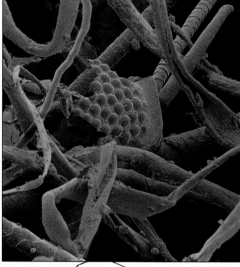

**Armchair dust**
*(x 700)*

Dirt is everywhere, even in the cleanest houses. It floats about in the air, landing on everything and piling up in the corners. It is made up of all sorts of junk. Specks of earth, pollen from flowers, tiny pieces of mould from food and flakes of human skin. It is a feast for the minute creatures which live in all houses.

*Flakes for every meal* (below). *Billions of tiny dust mites live in our beds, carpets and chairs. They are so small you cannot see them and no-one knew they were there until about 30 years ago. They munch away on flakes of human skin. Thousands of flakes rub off our bodies every time we roll over in bed, get dressed, move about or even stand still.*

Part of an insect's eye is tangled up amongst the hairs and fibres in this armchair dust.

**Dust mite**
*(x 850)*

**About 1,000,000 dust mites live in an ordinary single bed.**

## DID YOU KNOW?

Dust mites live in almost every house all over the world. They have been found 5,000m up on Mount Everest and even in the freezing Antarctic.

**Washing-up sponges**

(x 22)

Millions of
bacteria, like
these, grow on
the damp walls
of bathrooms
and kitchens.

*Swimming swarm.* These sponges may look clean, but
really they are all teeming with sausage-shaped bacteria.
These bacteria live anywhere that is warm and damp.
Washing-up sponges are perfect for them. They feast on
the tiny pieces of food which stick to the pads after they
have been used to wash up dirty plates and saucepans.
The creatures do not have arms and legs. They move over
a sponge by lashing their tails from side to side.

(x 950)

**Bacteria**
(x 3,000)

23

# Uninvited Guests

**Y**ou and your family may live in a house or a flat and you may think you are alone. But there are probably other lodgers sharing it with you. Some are so small you can't see them but you can sometimes see the holes they make if you look very closely. They have their homes in beds, in clothes, in the walls of the rooms, in wooden furniture and in food cupboards. There they are busy breeding, laying eggs, growing, eating and dying.

## Bedtime blues

Bedbugs are about 6mm long and are big enough to see easily. They are found all over the world, in birds' nests and in animal bedding as well as in beds.

Bedbugs feed on their hosts. They jab the long spike, or proboscis, on their heads into the skin of their victims and suck up their blood. In human beings, each jab makes a red, itchy spot.

**This bedbug has just had a good meal and its body is swollen with blood.**

*Snacking on sawdust* (below). Woodworm beetles are about 2mm long. They eat the dead wood of trees, wood in the roofs and ceilings of houses and wooden furniture.

*The female lays her eggs in early summer in cracks in wood. When the eggs hatch out, the grubs bore into the wood. They chew out tunnels for up to three years. Then they burrow a hole to the surface and come out as fully-grown adults. This exit hole is about 2mm across and may be the first sign of woodworm in your furniture. This adult woodworm beetle is just coming out of its hole.*

**Bedbug**
(x 60)

**Woodworm**
(x 30)

*Soup for starters* (right). Many different types of tiny beetle may infest food in cupboards and shops or stores. This one has munched its way into a packet of soup powder. Its jaws are so strong that it can chew through metal foil or plastic packing to reach its food. These beetles are too small to see but you can sometimes spot the holes they make where food spills out of a packet.

**Beetle**
(x 30)

**Grain weevil**
(x 27)

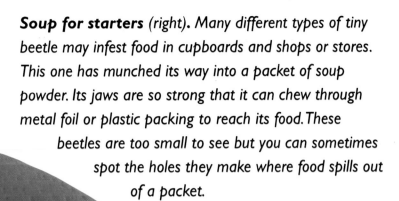

## DID YOU KNOW?

There are more than a million different types of insects. That is more than all the different types of other animals and plants in the world. And there may be billions or even trillions of insects in each different group.

This little monster (left) is a grain weevil. It is a beetle which feeds on grains of wheat. At the end of its long snout are sharp jaws, called mandibles. It bores through the hard husk of the grain and eats the floury insides.

A female grain weevil lives for nine months and lays up to 6,000 eggs.

25

# Pages on Paper

**Blotting paper**
*(x 150)*

**Filter paper**
*(x 500)*

**Tissue paper**
*(x 150)*

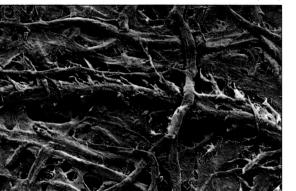

**Writing paper**
*(x 150)*

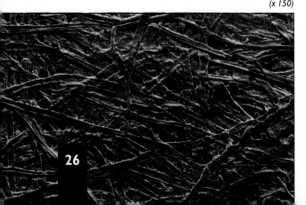

Next time you write something down or draw a picture, take a look at the paper you are using. You may just be able to see a fine texture on its surface. The texture is made by criss-crossing wood fibres, since most paper today is made from wood pulp. In the past, however, paper was made from other things. The Chinese used bamboo, rags and even old fishing nets, mashing them to a pulp. They spread the pulp out on flat bamboo sieves to dry in the sun. The rough sheets were then polished with stones.

*A forest of paper* (left). Paper-making begins with giant machines that chop specially-cut timber to a pulp. The pulp is cut up with lots of water, bleached to make it white and mixed with chemicals. The wood pulp is then spread out on huge sieves to drain off the water, pressed between rollers, dried and wound on enormous rolls.

Different types of paper are made with different chemicals and different amounts of wood pulp. Blotting paper is soft with open fibres to pick up the ink. Filter paper has open fibres to let liquids drain through. Tissue paper is made from very thin pulp. Writing paper is pressed between rollers to give it a hard, smooth surface.

**Very fine sandpaper, called glass paper, is used to smooth down wood. It is made of tiny pieces of glass glued to a tough sheet of paper.**

**Sandpaper**
*(x 25)*

**This is what happens when you use correcting fluid. A very close look** **shows the fluid covering the fibres of the paper and the ink marks.**

**Correcting fluid**
*(x 3)*

*(x 450)*

*Bursting bubbles* (below). Sticky paper notes that you can use again and again have a strip of bubbles on the back. The bubbles are resin filled with glue. When you press the paper down, some of the bubbles burst and let out the glue, making it sticky. You can pull off the paper note and press it down many times. When all the bubbles have been burst and the glue used up, the paper is no longer sticky.

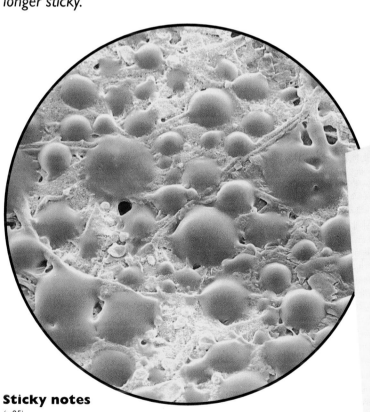

**Sticky notes**
*(x 85)*

# Making a Mark

Reeds, pointed sticks, metal rods and feathers have all been used for hundreds of years to write on paper. The word "pen" comes from the Latin word for feather. Goose feathers were often used and sharpened to a point with a penknife. Pens with steel nibs were first made about 200 years ago and fountain pens about 100 years ago.

Now we have a huge range of pens and pencils to write and draw with, using different types of ink. And there are many ways of printing books, magazines and newspapers with black ink and lots of colours.

**Ball-point pen**
(x 80)

*Fluorescent fibre-tip.* The nib of a felt-tip pen is a bundle of man-made fibres which are cut to give it its shape. Tiny spaces between the fibres hold the ink. More ink is stored in the tube of fibres inside the plastic holder. When you write, the ink in the nib comes out on the paper and more ink is sucked down the tube into the nib fibres.

A ball-point pen has a tiny ball at the tip. As you write with the pen, the ball rolls around inside the tube, picking up ink. The inky ball then rolls over the paper. The first really useful ball-point pen was invented by an artist called L. Biro, about 60 years ago.

**Felt-tip pen**
(x 1,500)

An ordinary pencil has enough lead in it to draw a line nearly 50km long.

The "lead" in a pencil is not made of lead at all. It is a mixture of graphite, a soft, black mineral, and clay which is baked hard. Different amounts of graphite can make the pencil lead hard or soft.

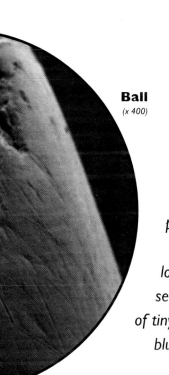

**Ball**
*(x 400)*

**Tip of lead pencil**
*(x 75)*

*Joining the dots.* *All the colour pictures in this book are printed with only three colours and black. If you look very closely at a picture, you can see it is made up of different amounts of tiny dots of colour. They are red, yellow, blue and black. Together they make up all the other different colours.*

**Colour printing dots**
*(x 20)*

*Before a book is printed, each colour photograph or picture is photographed with special filters or scanned electronically. This separates it into four pictures of one colour each. Four printing plates are made with the tiny dots from these pictures. When a book is printed on a huge machine, each plate is inked with one colour. The plates press, one at a time, on the paper, leaving a picture of coloured inky dots. When all four plates have printed their dots, the picture is complete.*

**Colour printing**

# Bathroom Basics

**Cotton bud**
*(x 500)*

Bathrooms often have things in them that are worth looking at closely. Many of them are made of made-made fibres in factories. Some are made of natural fibres, such as cotton, and come from different parts of the world. Some even grow under the sea.

The end of a cotton bud looks and feels very smooth. But when you look at it through a microscope, you can see that it is really made of rough, twisted cotton fibres.

**Bristles**
*(x 120)*

**Cotton buds**

*Tooth scrubbers.* The first toothbrushes had bristles of natural fibres and their handles were made of wood. Nowadays, most toothbrushes are made of man-made fibres, such as nylon. They last much longer and are much easier to keep clean. A surprising mixture of things go into the toothpaste we buy - finely powdered chalk, soapy detergent and glycerol, as well as sweeteners and flavourings. You can make your own toothpaste with baking soda, table salt and water.

This tooth-brush is old and worn. The bristles are coated with bits of food and dried toothpaste.

*(x 5)*

**Toothbrush**

**Natural sponge**
(x 8)

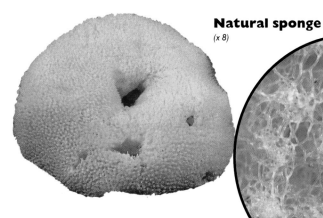

*Spongy skeleton.* *Natural sponges are made by tiny animals which live in warm sea water. Each one builds a skeleton of fibre with lots of holes in it. Water flows in and out of the holes, bringing food to the animals and taking away waste matter.*

*Natural sponges have been used for washing and cleaning for hundreds of years. In some places, they are still collected from the sea bed in their thousands by teams of sponge divers. Most of the sponges we use now, though, are synthetic. Synthetic sponges are made in factories out of man-made fibres such as nylon and polystyrene. Huge sheets of sponge are made that can then be cut into any size or shape. The sponge may be any colour or sheets of different colours sandwiched together.*

(x 200)

(x 100)

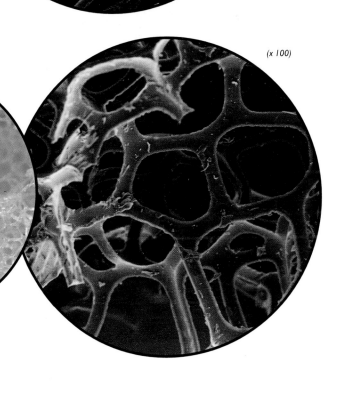

**Man-made sponge**
(x 6)

31

# Kitchen Curiosities

Kitchens are full of all sorts of interesting bits and pieces. There are probably more chemicals there than anywhere else in your house. That doesn't just mean detergents and cleansers - how about the blobs at the ends of matchsticks? Or the greyish crust you might see in your kettle? Both of these are chemicals too.

**Matches**

**Kettle fur**
(x 340)

***Crusty crystals*** *(above). The grey or white crust that often builds up inside our kettles is called "fur". It is made by a chemical which is always in water.*

*The chemical gets into the water when rain seeps through limestone rocks in the ground. The water runs into streams and rivers and reservoirs and, finally, comes out of the taps in your house. When the kettle is boiled, some of the water goes into the air as steam, leaving the chemical behind to build up slowly into piles of crystals.*

**Kettle**

**Burnt match head**
*(x 35)*

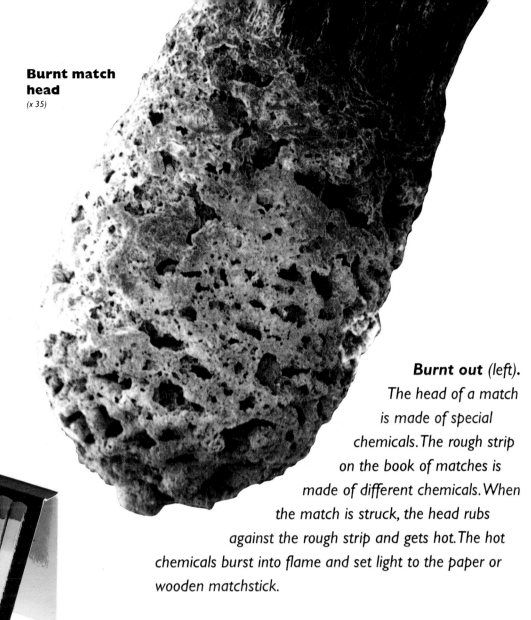

**Some pin boards are made of cork. Cork is the bark of evergreen oak trees which grow in Mediterranean countries, such as Spain and Portugal.**

**Pin**
*(x 12)*

***Burnt out*** *(left).*
*The head of a match is made of special chemicals. The rough strip on the book of matches is made of different chemicals. When the match is struck, the head rubs against the rough strip and gets hot. The hot chemicals burst into flame and set light to the paper or wooden matchstick.*

*Safety matches will only light if they are struck against the rough strip. Non-safety matches burst into flame if they are rubbed against anything rough, such as sandpaper or the sole of a shoe.*

**The bark is cut off the trees in long strips without harming them. The best bark is pressed, boiled in water and pressed again to make corks. The rest is ground up, mixed with oil and pressed into boards.**

**Pin board**
*(x 40)*

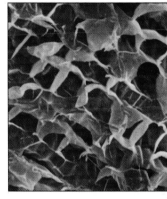

**Cork**
*(x 130)*

**A close-up of a book of matches shows that the striking strip is made of rough lumps of chemicals.**

**A long time ago, matches were made with gunpowder which exploded when struck.**

**Striking strip**
*(x 120)*

33

## Watch out!

Inside a watch, tiny wheels with teeth on the edges, called cogs, fit together. One is driven by a wound-up spring or, in a quartz watch, by a tiny electric motor. It turns the others, making them go round at the right speed to turn the hands on the watch's face.

# Odds and Ends

Lots of very ordinary things around the house are surprisingly complicated when you look at them through a microscope. You may already be familiar with the clever mechanisms inside watches, clocks and wind-up toys - but have you ever examined a musical instrument like a guitar and had a careful look at the strings that vibrate to make the sounds you hear?

*Notes on nylon* (below). *Cheap guitars have strings made of one strand of tightly-stretched nylon. On expensive guitars the strings are much more complicated.*

*The strings which make the low notes are bundles of lots of very fine strands of nylon. A thick strand of nylon is wrapped very tightly around the bundle. After a guitar has been played for a while, the strings get worn and have to be replaced.*

**Inside a watch**
(x 5)

**The face has been taken off this watch (above), showing all the different cogs behind it.**

**Guitar string**
(x 40)

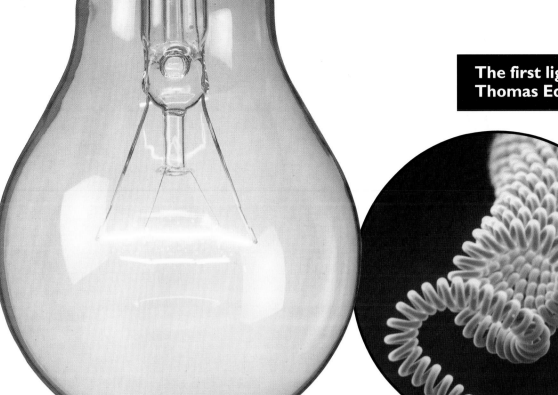

**Inside a light bulb**
(x 65)

**White hot.** Inside the glass of a light bulb are strips of metal, sticking out of a column of glass. Across the strips is a thin coil of wire, called the filament. This filament is made of a special metal called tungsten. Tungsten can get very hot without melting.

When you turn on a light, electricity goes along the wires into the bulb. It goes through the filament which starts to heat up very quickly. It gets hotter and hotter until it glows. The white light you see is the glowing filament. This makes the glass of the bulb hot.

**Filament**
(x 1,400)

**All the air is taken out of a light bulb to stop the filament burning away.**

# Guess What?

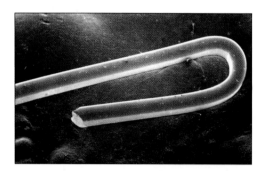

**1. Candy cane?** - this piece of stationery gets stuck through paper though, not on to your teeth.

**2. Electric liquorice** - you would need jaws of iron to bite through this wiry stuff.

**3. Take a peek** - if you looked over this fence, all you would see is a pile of soggy leaves.

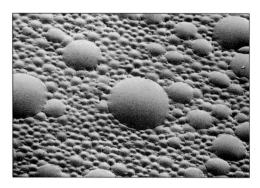

**4. Lunar landscape?** - many earthlings, in fact, like to put this in their sandwiches.

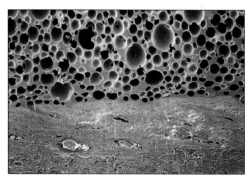

**5. Tough as an old boot** - one of these would definitely *not* make a tasty snack, however.

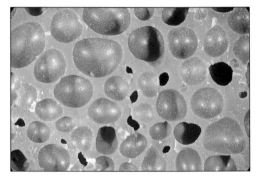

**6. A pool of bubbling mud?** - most people simply can't resist getting stuck into this.

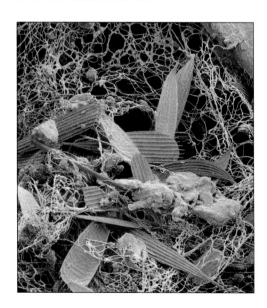

**7. Rope trick -** this may look thick and strong, but you wouldn't want to swing around on it.

**8. Whoops!** Has someone spilt their crisps? It's certainly cleaning time when this starts to build up.

1 end of staple (x 20)/2 insulated copper wire (x 35)/3 tea strainer (x 15)/ 4 mayonnaise (x 220)/5 leather and plastic sole of shoe/6 aerated chocolate (x 4)/7 strand of cotton (x 1,000)/8 moth wing scales amongst household dust (x 1,200).

# GLOSSARY

**Bacteria** - microscopic creatures that reproduce simply by dividing in two. There are thousands of different kinds of bacteria. Some are harmless, while others cause serious diseases in plants and animals.

**Compact disc** - a metal disc with a clear plastic coating. Microscopic pits in the metal contain different codes that represent the music. When the disc is played, a laser beam reads the codes and produces signals that are then translated to reproduce the original sounds.

**Dust mites** - minute creatures, too small to see, that live in all houses, feeding on the flakes of skin that we leave behind wherever we go.

**Filament** - the thin coil of metal inside a light bulb. When electricity passes through the filament, it heats up very quickly, becoming so hot that it glows white and makes light.

**Graphite** - a soft black mineral used in pencil lead. Graphite forms in layers that are only weakly linked together; when you write or draw with a pencil, layers of graphite break away and stick to the page.

**Hallmark** - a special set of marks stamped on things made of gold or silver. The hallmark tells you how much silver or gold has been used, who made the object and when and where it was tested for purity.

**Kettle fur** - the chalky crust that forms in kettles. It is made of a chemical called calcium carbonate, which is found in water. As the water in the kettle boils away, some of the chemical is left behind.

**Laser beam** - a narrow beam of intense energy. The beam can be used to burn through solid objects and can travel a long way without spreading out like ordinary light. Lasers can burn holes in metal, measure great distances and even be used in surgical operations.

**Man-made fibres** - fibres made from oil and other chemicals. They are hard-wearing and often stronger than natural fibres. Nylon, acrylic and polyester are all man-made fibres.

**Microchip** - a tiny, paper-thin slice of silicon, no bigger than a fingernail, that has been printed with electrical circuits. The circuits can pass on or store electronic signals.

**Moulds** - tiny fungi that grow on food when it is warm and damp. Some moulds spoil food, but some can be useful. The special taste of "blue" cheese comes from a mould that is deliberately put into it.

**Natural fibres** - fibres produced by plants and animals that can be spun and then knitted or woven to make cloth. Cotton and wool are both natural fibres.

**Printed circuit board** - a board printed with a metal pattern that carries electricity to microchips and switches fixed to the board. Printed circuit boards make it easy to assemble electrical equipment.

**Scanning** - one way to reproduce pictures in a book or magazine. A scanner converts the colours in a picture into electronic signals.

**Sound waves** - vibrations in the air caused by making a noise, such as banging a drum. The sound waves reach your ear and make your ear drum vibrate; your brain picks up the signal and you hear the sound.

**Stylus** - a special needle used with records. It follows the grooves in the record, making the stylus vibrate. The vibrations are turned into electrical signals, which come out through the speakers to reproduce the original sound.

**Woodworm** - the young grubs of tiny beetles that eat wooden furniture and the wood in the roofs and ceilings of houses. They also eat the dead wood of trees.

**Yeast** - a tiny fungus used to make wine, because it converts sugar into alcohol. Yeast is also used to make bread. In the warm, wet dough, the yeast gives off a gas called carbon dioxide; the gas forms bubbles, which make the dough swell up and rise.

# INDEX

# ACKNOWLEDGEMENTS

The authors and publishers would like to thank Andrew Syred of Microscopix, Liz Hirst at the National Institute of Medical Research and Steve Gorton for their assistance in the preparation of this book, as well as the other photographers and organisations listed below for their kind permission to reproduce the following photographs:

**Dr Tony Brain**; 8 centre and bottom left, 10 left of centre, 11 top right and bottom right, 16 bottom right, 17 top left, above centre and top right, 21 top left and top right, 25 top right, 28 top right, 28-29, 29 above centre, 33 top right, right of centre and bottom right, 35 top right and right of centre, 36 right of centre, back cover top left

**British Leather Confederation**; 36 centre

**David Burder**; 20-21 bottom

**Steve Gorton**; front cover left and right, 5 centre, 6 top left, 7 below centre, 9 bottom, 10-11 bottom, 12-13 bottom, 14-15 top, 16 centre, 17 bottom right, 18 top, 18-19 bottom, 21 right of centre, 23 top left, 30 right of centre, 32 bottom left, 32-33 centre, 34 bottom left, 34-35 bottom, 35 top left, back cover bottom right

**Liz Hirst/NIMR**; 12-13 centre, 26 top left, below centre left and bottom left

**Science Photo Library**; 9 top, 13 bottom right, 27 bottom left, 34 left of centre /**Biophoto Associates**; front cover centre, 15 top left, above centre and top right, 25 bottom /**Dr Tony Brain**; 18 above centre and bottom, 24 bottom left /**Dr Tony Brain and David Parker**; 6 right, 24 bottom right /**Dr Jeremy Burgess**; 3 bottom, 5 left and right, 6 left of centre and bottom left, 9 centre, 13 top right and right of centre, 15 bottom right, 17 left of centre, 18 centre, 19 top left, 20 left, 26 bottom right, 32 centre, 36 left of centre /**Stevie Grand**; 4 bottom left /**John Heseltine**; 27 bottom right /**R E Litchfield**; 11 centre, 36 bottom right /**Sidney Moulds**; 3 right of centre, 10 bottom left /**David Scharf**; 3, 13 centre, 22 top right, 22-23 bottom, 23 top right, right of centre and bottom right, 29 bottom right, 36 bottom left / **Sheila Terry**; 21 bottom right /**Jeremy Trew**; 4 top left

**Tony Stone Worldwide/B S Turner**; 7 above centre

**Andrew Syred/Microscopix**; 4 top right, right of centre, bottom right and below centre, 7 top right and bottom right, 11 left of centre, 14 centre, 15 bottom left, 16 bottom left, 26 below centre left, 27 top and above centre right, 28 bottom left and below centre, 29 top right and right of centre, 30 top right, left of centre, bottom left and bottom right, 31 top left, above centre, right of centre, bottom right, below centre and bottom left, 33 top left and bottom, 34 bottom right, 36 top left, above centre, and top right, back cover above centre, right of centre, below centre right and bottom left

**All illustrations by Jane Gedye**

40